Thoughts and Quotes from America's
most assured leader©

John William Scott

TRUMP *isms*®

TRUMPisms®

Author: Scott, John William

ISBN: 978-164-858-1496

TRUMP *isms*®

Never has there been a more iconic and divisive figure in American Politics and business. Donald Trump is a business man, TV celebrity, and a world leader and politician. He has gone from an average American home to riches, stardom and finally into the most powerful office in the world, President of the United States.

People do not have to guess or speculate about what he thinks. He just says it. If you don't like him, he doesn't care, if he doesn't like you, he will say it. To say he has no filter of what he thinks to what he says would be an understatement. It is this very quality that makes him such a polarizing figure.

From young and brash to billionaire, from pompous to president, he believes he can, he let's everyone know he can and he does. He has built businesses, skyscrapers, golf courses and resorts all worldwide. He has upset the political apple cart. Trump's made the world more controversial and candid by just being himself and just being in it. Is it better? *You decide.*

Whether you like Trump or not, whoever you are, you cannot deny that he believes he can do what he wants and will do what he says. Enjoy his thoughts and beliefs and learn life lessons from his towering achievements.

John William Scott – An American

TRUMP*isms*®

You have to think anyway, so why not think BIG?

My whole life is about winning. I don't lose often.

If you love what you do, it keeps you young and energized.

Make your work more pleasurable.

We need strength, we need energy,

we need brain in this country to turn it around.

Get in, get it done, get it done right and get out.

We're a nation that speaks English. I think that, while we're in this nation, we should be speaking English. That's how we assimilate.

Without passion you don't have energy.

Without energy you have nothing.

TRUMP*isms*®

I'm competitive,
and I love
to create
challenges
for myself.
That's not always
a good thing.
It can make life
complicated.

I will fight for you
with every breath
in my body – and
I will never, ever
let you down.

Nothing is easy. But who wants nothing?

We will make
America strong
again.
We will make
America proud
again.
We will make
America safe again.
And we will make
America great
again.

It's always good to be underestimated.

When somebody challenges you, fight back.

I have a great relationship with people.

You do your job,
you keep
your job.
Do it well,
you get
a better job.

I own guns.
Fortunately,
I have never had
to use them,
but, believe me,
I feel a lot safer
knowing that
they are there.

You can quote me but only as a source close to Donald.

We must speak
our minds openly,
debate our
disagreements
honestly, but
always pursue
solidarity.

What separates
the winners from
the losers is how
a person reacts
to each new twist
of fate.

Turn trying times into triumphs.

Money was never
a big motivation
for me, except
as a way
to keep score.

I never
withdraw.
I've never
withdrawn
in my life.

Sometimes you need conflict in order to come up with a solution.

I'm aggressive,
but I also get
things done.

TRUMP *isms*®

Free advice
tends to be worth
what you pay
for it.

Through weakness, often times, you can't make the right sort of settlement.

I judge people
based on
their capability,
honesty,
and merit.

Part of being
a winner is
knowing when
enough is
enough.

Sometimes you have to give up the fight and walk away, and move on to something that's more productive.

I don't like losers.

In the end, you're measured not by how much you undertake but by what you finally accomplish.

No dream is too big.

The U.S. has become a dumping ground for everybody else's problems.

Until you start,
you won't know
where the
problems will
occur. You won't
have the
experience to solve
them. Instead, get
into action, and
solve the problems
as they arise.

TRUMP*isms*®

A lot of people actually don't know how to win.

There is no global anthem, no global currency, no certificate of global citizenship, we pledge allegiance to one flag and that flag is the American Flag!

I know how to stand my ground.

If you get good ratings, they'll cover you even if you have nothing to say.

If people can just
pour into the
country illegally,
you don't have
a country.

I try to learn from the past.

Everything I do in life is framed through the view of a businessman. That's my instinct.

I was a great student.
I was good at everything.

You can't be too greedy.

TRUMP *isms*®

Any system that
discourages work,
discourages
productivity,
discourages
economic
progress,
is wrong.

Every day, I wake up determined to deliver a better life for the people all across this nation that have been neglected, ignored, and abandoned.

TRUMP*isms*®

I have visited the laid-off factory workers and the communities crushed by our horrible and unfair trade deals. These are the forgotten men and women of our country.

The most basic duty of government is to defend the lives of its own citizens. Any government that fails to do so is a government unworthy to lead.

Immigration
is a privilege.

Sometimes your best investments are the ones you don't make.

I always look at it that I work with my employees as opposed to them working for me.

We will follow two simple rules: Buy American and hire American.

Do not let anyone tell you it cannot be done.

No challenge can match the heart and fight and spirit of America.

We will not fail.

TRUMP*isms*®

The only people
bullies push
around are the
ones they know
they can beat.

60

Our country will thrive and prosper again.

People are tired
of seeing
politicians
as all talk
and no action.

I've been making deals all my life.

My father would always praise me.

TRUMP *isms*®

I don't make
deals for the
money.
I've got enough.
I do it to do it.

I give
to everybody.
When I need
something from
them two years
later, three years
later, I call them,
they are there
for me.

I've met some
great people
that deal with me
in the press.
I've also met
some people
that were very
dishonorable.

A great leader has to be savvy at negotiations.

TRUMP*isms*®

I was born
with the drive
for success.

I wasn't satisfied
just to earn
a good living.
I was looking
to make
a statement.

I have an attention span that's as long as it has to be.

What matters is the doing.

TRUMP *isms*®

You can learn a lot about a person. It's not that they have to sink the putt and there's a great deal of talent involved. But you do learn about how competitive a person is on the golf course, and frankly, how honest.

I always want to
think of myself
as an underdog.

You will always be second guessed, that's what people do.

The way I run my business seems to be easier than the way I run my life.

In real life, if I were firing you… you want to let them down as lightly as possible. I'd tell you what a great job you did, how fantastic you are, and how you can do better someplace else.

No dream is too big.

If your boss is a sadist, then you have a big problem. In that case, fire your boss and get a new job.

My job is not to
represent the
world. My job is
to represent the
United States of
America.

Good people don't go into government.

It's not a very pleasant thing. I don't like firing people.

When America is united, America is totally unstoppable.

A little more
moderation
would be good.

We will bring back our jobs. We will bring back our borders. We will bring back our wealth. And we will bring back our dreams.

Listen to your gut, no matter how good something sounds on paper.

We need a certain toughness in this country, or we're going to end up like a lot of the other places, and we're not going to have a country left.

Experience taught me a few things. One is that you're generally better off with what you know.

There is no beating around the bush.

I have made the tough decisions, always with an eye toward the bottom line.

It's time America was run like a business.

if I'm forced
to fight for
something I
really care about,
I will never,
ever back down.

I'm a bit of a
P. T. Barnum.
I make stars
out of everyone.

This is the time to make the great deal.

The debt limits have to come down. The whole world of debt has to be changed as far as this country is concerned.

Make America great again.

We have to create jobs and we have to create them rapidly because if we don't things are just going to head in a direction that's going to be almost impossible to recover from.

If you don't trust, you're not going to do very well.

They don't like it when somebody such as myself speaks the truth.

TRUMP *isms* ®

Our politicians are stupid.

I think the big problem this country has is being politically correct.

If you don't tell people about your success, they probably won't know about it.

I don't think you could be a politician if you didn't shake hands.

People are so shocked when they find out I go to church, and I love God.

TRUMP*isms*®

The Pope, I hope, can only be scared by God.

So many people
are on television
that don't know
me, and yet
they're
experts on me.

I go to Washington and I see all these politicians, and I see "the swamp", and it's not a good place, in fact, we ought to change it from the word 'swamp' to the word 'cesspool'.

TRUMP*isms*®

Everybody has their detractors.

I only have one thing in mind, and that's doing a great job for the country.

I'm worth far too
much money.
I don't need
anybody's
money.

I'm going to keep Social Security without change, except I'm going to get rid of the waste, fraud, and abuse; same thing with Medicare.

I've been dealing
with politicians
all my life.
And I've always
gotten them to do
what I need
them to do.

Be a firm and fair trader.

There's nothing I can hide. That's me. Television brings out your flaws, your weaknesses, your strengths, and your truths. The audience either likes you or it doesn't.

I've always felt
the need to pray.
This office is so
powerful that
you need God
even more.

You don't get a standing ovation and get boos. They don't go hand in hand.

You have an instinct and you go with it. Especially when it comes to deal-making.

Either you're good at it or you're not.

Once you dig that foundation - and you secure that foundation, that building isn't going anywhere.

I have made some really significant deals because I play golf.

There's always opposition when you do something big.

I work in the
toughest
business, and
I do it in the
toughest city.
I deal with
ruthless people.

You learn a lot about people playing golf: their integrity, how they play under pressure.

Nothing we want for our future is beyond our reach.

Growth is an indication of life.

TRUMP *isms*®

There is only one core issue in the immigration debate and it is this: the well-being of the American people. Nothing even comes a close second.

There are a lot of foolish people.

No challenge is too great.

I can't believe I'm saying I'm a politician.

People that really
succeed in life
are those that
don't quit.

The problems we face now - will last only as long as we continue relying on the same politicians who created them in the first place.

There can be no prosperity without law and order.

I have a message for the terrorists trying to kill our citizens: we will find you, we will destroy you.

I'm great with debt, nobody knows debt better than me. I made a fortune by using debt. And if things don't work out I renegotiate the debt, I mean that's a smart thing not a stupid thing.

I have no
patience
for injustice,
no tolerance
for government
incompetence,
no sympathy for
leaders who fail
their citizens.

Every action I take, I will ask myself, *'Does this make life better for Americans'.*

Be considerate and compassionate to everyone.

Together, we will determine the course of America and the world for years to come.

Everyone in golf is nice.

We will face challenges. We will confront hardships. But we will get the job done.

What truly
matters is not
which party
controls our
government,
but whether
our government
is controlled
by the people.

The forgotten men and women of our country will be forgotten no longer.

Americans want good jobs for themselves. These are the just and reasonable demands of a righteous public.

America First.

TRUMP *isms*®

I refuse to be
politically
correct.

We do not seek to
impose our way
of life on anyone,
but rather to let
it shine as
an example
for everyone
to follow.

Never think of
learning as being
a burden or
studying as
being boring.

I don't frankly have time for total political correctness. And to be honest with you, this country doesn't have time either.

We will seek friendship and goodwill with the nations of the world.

The harder I work, the luckier I get.

Whether we are black, brown, yellow or white, we all bleed the same red blood of patriots, we all enjoy the same glorious freedoms, and we all salute the same great American Flag.

To all Americans, in every city near and far, small and large, from mountain to mountain, and from ocean to ocean, hear these words: YOU WILL NEVER BE IGNORED AGAIN.

Nothing great in the world has been accomplished without passion.

Courage is not the absence of fear.

There is no such
thing as an
unrealistic goal–
just unrealistic
time frames.

TRUMP*isms*®

Criticism is
easier to take
when you realize
that the only
people who
aren't criticized
are those who
don't take risks.

Rules are meant to be broken.

When you have momentum going, play the momentum.

My philosophy is always to hire the best from the best.

The men and women
of our military are
totally loyal to our
country. And every
day I am President,
America will always
be totally
loyal to you.

I think I've seen every type of person there is that God created.

A nation 'without borders' is not a nation at all.

The rule of law matters.

People who think achieving success is a linear A-to-Z process, a straight shot to the top, simply aren't in touch with reality.

The more government takes in taxes, the less incentive people have to work.

Any system that penalizes success and accomplishment is wrong.

TRUMP *isms*®

If you reduce tax rates and allow people to spend or save more of what they earn, they'll be more industrious; The result... more prosperity for all ... and more revenue for government.

**Get going.
Move forward.
Aim High.
Plan a takeoff.
Don't just sit on
the runway and
hope someone will
come along and
push the airplane.**

Change your attitude and gain some altitude.

We are responsible for our own luck.

It doesn't hurt to get more education.

Don't get sidetracked. If you do get sidetracked, get back on track. Ultimately sidetracking kills you.

Can you imagine if you didn't have me?

I discovered, for the first time but not the last, that politicians don't care too much what things cost. It's not their money.

Good publicity is preferable to bad, bad publicity is sometimes better than no publicity at all.

Success appears to happen overnight because we see stories on TV about unknown people who suddenly become famous. Just because a television crew one day decides to do a story doesn't mean it didn't exist before.

We must protect
our borders.
Protection will
lead to great
prosperity
and strength.

Watch, listen, and learn.
You can't know it all yourself.
Anyone who thinks they do is destined for mediocrity.

My style of deal-making is quite simple. I aim very high, and then I just keep pushing and pushing and pushing to get what I'm after.

Critics get to say what they want to about my work, so why shouldn't I be able to say what I want to about theirs?

There's an old German proverb;

"Fear makes the wolf bigger than he is,"

and that is true.

At some point I may be wrong and at some point I may be right.

We will no longer
surrender this
country or its
people to the
false song
of globalism.

My motto is: Always get even. When somebody screws you, screw them back in spades.

Success comes from failure, not from memorizing the right answers.

TRUMP *isms*®

Our country,
our people,
and our laws,
our top priority.

I don't hire a lot
of number-
crunchers,
and I don't trust
fancy marketing
surveys.
I do my own
surveys
and draw my own
conclusions.

People may not always think big themselves, but they can get very excited by those who do.

Leverage: don't make deals without it.

What's the point of having great knowledge and keeping it all to yourself?

If you are a little different, or a little outrageous, or if you do things that are bold or controversial, the press is going to write about you.

When people are
in a focused
state, the words
"I can't," "I'll try,"
"maybe" and "I'll
do it tomorrow,"
get forced out
of their
vocabularies.

I grew up in New York City, a town with different races, religions, and peoples.
It breeds tolerance.

A government big
enough to give
you everything
you want is a
government big
enough to take
from you
everything
you have.

You always have
an opportunity.

There's always
an opportunity.

Partnerships must have loyalty and integrity.

Sheer persistence is the difference between success and failure.

Luck does not
come around
often. So when it
does, be sure to
take full
advantage of it.

The worst things
in history have
happened when
people stop
thinking for
themselves.

I like to think of the word "FOCUS" as;

F-ollow

O-ne

C-ourse

U-ntil

S-uccessful

Do not spend too much time planning or trying to anticipate and solve problems before they happen. That is just another kind of excuse for procrastination.

When luck is on your side it is not the time to be modest or timid. It is the time to go for the biggest success you can possibly achieve.

Make an effort to get to know people.

Learn their names.

A great leader has to be flexible, holding his ground on the major principles but finding room for compromises that can bring people together.

Governments cannot create real jobs. Only entrepreneurs can do that.

A brand is two words: the 'Promise' you telegraph, and the 'Experience' you deliver.

The biggest little thing; A lifelong commitment to education.

Without straightforward feedback, entrepreneurs cannot make sound decisions.

TRUMP *isms*®

I have a very simple
rule when it comes to
management:
Hire the best people
from your
competitors, pay them
more than they were
earning, and give
them bonuses and
incentives based on
their performance.
That's how you build a
first-class operation.

Your business,
and your brand
must first let
people know
what you care
about and that
you care
about them.

The more predictable the business, the more valuable it is.

Focus is essential to success, and successful people are people who can focus.

You have to leave your comfort zone.

You don't reward failure by promoting those responsible for it, because all you get is more failure.

Learn something new every day.

If you try once,
you should try
again. Keep that
focus exactly
where it should
be, on winning.

Be open to new information and ideas.

Always think positively and expect the best.

**Stay confident
even when
something
bad happens.
It is just a bump
in the road.
It will pass.**

The future belongs to those who believe.

Make every day extraordinary no matter what your job is.

TRUMP*isms*®

I've said some
foolish things,
but there is
a difference
between words
and actions.

222

We are guided by outcomes, not ideology.

Use your work to better yourself.

If you have laws that you don't enforce, then you don't have laws.

TRUMP*isms*®

Once you focus on
your life's objectives,
you need to focus on
your instructors to
make sure they are
qualified to teach you
what you want
to know.
They should have
already been where
you want to go
and have lived
to tell about it.

You're paid
to get it right.

Just remember what you're seeing and what you're reading is not always what's happening.

The constitutional right to defend yourself doesn't stop at the end of your driveway.

It takes just as much time to close a big deal as it does to close a small deal.

Treat the word "impossible" as nothing more than motivation.

It's next to
impossible
to build
a successful
business without
relationships.

Operate your day-to-day business as if bad times are always here.

TRUMP*isms*®

Socialism is
about only one
thing. It's called
power for the
ruling class.
That's what it is.

Have the courage to speak the truth, to do what is right, and to fight for what you believe.

I've always won, and I'm going to continue to win. And that's the way it is.

You must work on
improving your
skills every day.

It is easier to
finance a big
deal. Bankers
would much
rather lend
money for a big
project than for
a small one.

See both sides of the story and work towards a mutually beneficial situation for everyone.

Sometimes you have to toot your own horn because nobody else is going to do it for you.

If you can't get excited about what you are doing, how can you expect anyone else to?

We must choose to Believe in America. History is watching us now.

Expect the unexpected!

Keep moving forward at all times.

Talent is more important than experience.

Problems are often opportunities coming at us in packaging that isn't what we expected.

The worst thing you can possibly do in a deal is seem desperate to make it.

Leverage is having something the other guy wants. Or better yet, needs.

Sometimes understanding other people's problems is the key to finding opportunities.

Take the pains required to become what you want to become, or you might end up becoming something you'd rather not be.

Open markets are the ideal, but if one guy is cheating the whole time, how is that free trade?

The problems we face now – will last only as long as we continue relying on the same politicians who created them in the first place.

If you plan for the worst, If you can live with the worst, the good will always take care of itself.

You cannot stand still. If you do, life will pass you by.

A pro looks at the people, because they know business is about people.

We are responsible for ourselves.

If you see
responsibility
as a bum deal,
then you are
not seeing it for
what it really is,
a great
opportunity.

Use your mind
to visualize how
things might be.
That can make
the plethora
of details and
setbacks just a
part of the plan.

If you can accept losing, you already lost.

Following your convictions means you must be willing to face criticism from those who lack the same courage to do what is right.

When the pilgrims landed at Plymouth they prayed. When the Founders wrote the Declaration of Independence, they invoked our creator four times, because in America we don't worship government, we worship God.

Demand the best from yourself and be totally unafraid to challenge entrenched interests and failed power structures.

Instead of trying to
deflect problems or
obstacles and send
them off in another
direction,
try to embrace
them.

TRUMP*isms*®

Don't get
too attached
to your ideas.
Adjust, adapt,
and take things
in stride.

To be successful,
a person must
learn to fail,
correct, learn,
apply what
was learned,
and fail again.

The future belongs to the people who follow their heart no matter what the critics say, because they truly believe in their vision.

Drain the swamp!

I try not to schedule too many meetings.

If it can't be fun,

What's the point?

I keep my options open.

If the premium is big enough, I'll sell.

I hate lawsuits,
but the fact is
that if you're
right, you've got
to take a stand
or people will
walk all over you.

I always take calls from my kids, no matter what I am doing.

Never waste time.

I won't let my personal preferences affect my business judgement.

When I do an interview, I always keep it short.

Be very conservative in business.

I always go into the deal anticipating the worst.

I try never to leave myself too exposed.

Protect yourself by being flexible.

I'm a great
believer
in asking
everyone for
an opinion
before
I make a
decision.

I ask and I ask
and I ask until
I begin to get
a gut feeling
about something.

I have learned much more from conducting my own random surveys than I could ever have learned from the greatest of consulting firms.

People I don't take too seriously are the critics.

I always make it a point to ask cab drivers questions.

You have to convince the other guy it's in his interest to make the deal.

You don't
necessarily need
the best location.
You need the
best deal.

You can have the
most wonderful
product in the
world, but if
people don't
know about it, it's
not going to be
worth much.

One thing I've
learned about
the press is that
they're always
hungry for a good
story. The more
sensational
the better.

I've always done things a little differently.

When I talk to
reporters, I try
to be straight.
I try not to
deceive them or
be too defensive.

The way
I promote
is bravado.
I play to people's
fantasies.

Much as it pays to emphasize the positive, there are times when the only choice is confrontation.

I'm very good to people who are good to me.

If you're fighting
for something
you believe in,
things usually
work out for the
best in the end.

You can't con
people, at least
not for long.

If you don't
deliver the
goods, people
will eventually
catch on.

Ask for something extraordinary.

**Business is full
of people who
talk a good game
but don't deliver.**

The dollar always talks in the end.

I believe in spending what you have to, but I also believe in not spending more than you should.

No, I'm not going to give you a question, you are FAKE NEWS.

Every penny counts, because before too long your pennies turn into dollars.

Small jobs get out of control if you're not attentive.

Life is very fragile and success doesn't change that.

Anything can change without warning.

I don't spend a lot of time worrying.

The most important influence on me growing up was my father.

I apologize
when I'm wrong.

The most important thing in life is to love what you're doing, because that's the only way you'll ever be really good at it.

I plan for the future by focusing exclusively on the present.

People either like me a lot or they do not like me at all.

Know what everything costs.

Never stand in front of someone's door when you knock.

Success becomes a matter of marketing and management.

It's not how many
hours you put in,
it's what you get
done while your
working
the hours.

Stealing is the worst.

You can't
be scared.

Next to loyalty, toughness is the most important thing.

I am basically an optimist.

The simplest approach is often the most effective.

If you want to buy something, it's obviously in your best interest to convince the seller that what he's got isn't worth much.

**Anyone can
bid anything.
Particularly
when there
are all sorts of
contingencies.**

If I was going to attract attention, I had to raise my profile.

You need advertising most, when people aren't buying.

I try to keep risk to an absolute minimum.

A good looking presentation goes a long ways.

Sheer persistence is the difference between success and failure.

Sometimes making a deal comes down to timing.

Things always turn around.

The New York
Stock Exchange
happens to
be the biggest
casino
in the world.

The worst of times often create the best opportunities.

There are always buyers for the best.

Negotiate very reasonable prices.

A deal is a deal.
I live up to what
I've agreed to.

The smarter guys understand that while big revenues are great, the real issue is the spread between the revenues and costs, because that's your profit.

There are times when you have to be aggressive, but there are also times when your best strategy is to lie back.

I fight when I feel I'm getting screwed, even if it's costly and difficult and risky.

The only person I have to please is myself.

For too long, a small group in our nation's capital has reaped the rewards of government while the people have borne the cost.

It pays to trust your instincts.

"Modest" is not my favorite word.

Committees are what insecure people create in order to put off making hard decisions.

I like consultants
even less than
I like
committees.

My attitude is
that you can't get
hurt by asking.

You do your best and if it doesn't work, you move on to the next thing.

I just got fed up
one day and
decided to
do something
about it.

If there's one thing
I've learned from
dealing with
politicians over
the years, it's
that the only thing
guaranteed to force
them into action
is the press.
More specifically,
the fear of the press.

The cure cannot be bigger than the problem.

TRUMP *isms* ®

Bullies may
act tough,
but they're really
closet cowards.

Courage is the
ability to act
effectively,
in spite of fear.

Sometimes by losing a battle you find a new way to win the war.

Objective qualifying standards ought to be; Provable past performance.

You can get any
job done through
sheer force
of will.

People have been watching for years to watch me fall. I'm not about to help the cause.

When I can, I tell the truth.

One of the first things that anyone should learn about real estate, is never sign a letter of intent.

The key is to find
mutual interest.
Deals work best
when each side
gets something
it wants
from the other.

Find a way
to immediately
capture
the public
imagination.

I can be irritated all I want and it won't do any good.

Dishonesty
is intolerable.

As hard as I push, in the end I'm practical.

Providing jobs is a far more constructive solution than creating welfare programs.

If a project is going to move forward, there has to be some spirit of cooperation.

When you open
your heart
to patriotism,
there is no room
for prejudice.

I don't go out of my way to be cordial to enemies.

The more people
tell you it's not
possible, that it
can't be done, the
more you should
be absolutely
determined to
prove them
wrong.

Giving time is far more valuable than just giving money.

Keep all options open, it's the only way you truly protect yourself.

Anyone who
thinks my story
is anywhere
near over is
sadly mistaken.

TRUMP *isms*®

ABOUT THE AUTHOR: John W. Scott is the son of a World War II survivor. His mother lived through Hitler's regime in German occupied Norway in the 1940's. Her family immigrated by boat to the U.S. and entered through Ellis Island and the Statute of Liberty. His Father, fought in the Korean War. His great, great grandfather fought in the civil war. His ancestor fought in the revolutionary war with Washington at Yorktown against the British. Both parents taught him a patriot's love of this country and it's history.

John is a former High School history teacher, and college instructor. He has written two college text books and has published dozens of educational books and articles.   He has been captivated by the brash bold actions and words of Donald Trump. Sometimes laughing in disbelief and horror and other times crying in appreciation and admiration. John has read hundreds of books and articles on Trump to produce this work. His goal was to show the beliefs, attitudes and aptitudes of one of America's most accomplished men. John is happily married to his wife Monnika and they reside in South Jordan, Utah.

TRUMPisms©
John W. Scott
PO Box 95450 South Jordan, UT.
84095 USA

A GREAT GIFT with a Lifetime of Lessons

371

Made in the USA
Coppell, TX
07 September 2020

37206111R10203